FLUTE

Hal•Leonard
INSTRUMENTAL
PLAY-ALONG

CONTENTS

To access audio visit:
www.halleonard.com/mylibrary

Enter Code
6821-8958-3016-2362

Audio Arrangements by Peter Deneff

ISBN 978-1-4950-0553-4

HAL•LEONARD®
CORPORATION

7777 W. BLUEMOUND RD. P.O. BOX 13819 MILWAUKEE, WI 53213

Visit Hal Leonard Online at
www.halleonard.com

BATMAN THEME

FLUTE

Music by
NEAL HEFTI

GABRIEL'S OBOE

from the Motion Picture THE MISSION

FLUTE

Music by
ENNIO MORRICONE

THE GODFATHER
(Love Theme)
from the Paramount Picture THE GODFATHER

FLUTE

By NINO ROTA

LAST OF THE MOHICANS
(Main Theme)

from the Twentieth Century Fox Motion Picture THE LAST OF THE MOHICANS

FLUTE

By TREVOR JONES

GONNA FLY NOW
Theme from ROCKY

FLUTE

Words by CAROL CONNORS and AYN ROBBINS
Music by BILL CONTI

HE'S A PIRATE

from Walt Disney Pictures' PIRATES OF THE CARIBBEAN:
THE CURSE OF THE BLACK PEARL

FLUTE

Music by
KLAUS BADELT

MRS. DARCY
from PRIDE AND PREJUDICE

FLUTE

By DARIO MARIANELLI

MY HEART WILL GO ON
(Love Theme from 'TITANIC')
from the Paramount and Twentieth Century Fox Motion Picture TITANIC

Flute

Music by JAMES HORNER
Lyric by WILL JENNINGS

NOW WE ARE FREE

from the Dreamworks film GLADIATOR

Flute

Written by HANS ZIMMER,
LISA GERRARD and KLAUS BADELT

OVER THE RAINBOW

from THE WIZARD OF OZ

Flute

Music by HAROLD ARLEN
Lyric by E.Y. "Yip" HARBURG

THE PINK PANTHER

from THE PINK PANTHER

Flute

By HENRY MANCINI

STAR WARS
(Main Theme)
from STAR WARS, THE EMPIRE STRIKES BACK and RETURN OF THE JEDI

Flute

Music by
JOHN WILLIAMS